The piano pieces for CHILDREN
For Small Hands-No Octaves

こどものためのピアノ曲集

音のメルヘン

石井 歓 作曲

FABLES BY MUSIC
composed by Kan Ishii

edition KAWAI

音楽を　愛するこころ
　　そこに
　　　　人間の証しが在る

　そのようなこころは，幼ない時期に芽生え
るもののようです。

　この曲集は，生々と躍動する〈リズム〉，
今日から明日に向って必要な，新鮮な〈音感
覚〉を基調とし，更に，右，左，両手の均衡
がとれた練習と，音楽的美感覚を高めること
を目的に作曲されたものであります。

　曲集の後半には，演奏会などにも用いられ
るよう，演奏効果を考慮した作品を用意して
あります。

　私にとって，未開発であったこの分野，〈童
画のように，美しいせかい〉に眼を向けさせ，
かつ，非情なまでの督促に，それこそ尻をた
たかれる思いで一曲一曲を作曲していった時
を思い出し，完成した今日，カワイ出版の上野
一郎さんはじめ若い人々の熱意に感謝したい
のです。

1979年10月

石井　歓

A world together,
With a man's heart love of music
Which helps to fulfil his life.

　This kind of heart usually learns to bloom at an early age.

　These pieces are composed on the bases of lively rhythms together with a fresh sense of modern music. A balanced practice to the use of both the right and left hand has purposely been included, with the intention of also widening a sense of musical aesthetics.

　The second half of these compositions may well be suitable for concert playing, since they are not only enjoyable to play but also pleasing to listen to.

October 1979,

Kan Ishii

もくじ　CONTENTS

1　小犬とおさんぽ …………………………… 4 ……………………………… Walking with My Puppy

2　だんだん 石だん …………………………… 5 ……………………………… Up and Down The Steps

3　ゆきみちのおつかい ……………………… 6 ……………………………… The Snowy Pathway

4　おいかけっこ ……………………………… 8 ……………………………… Let's Play Tag!

5　ペンギンちゃんがやってくる …………… 9 ……………………………… The Penguins are Coming

6　小リスのトランポリン …………………… 10 ……………………………… A Baby Squirrel on A Trampolin

7　ゆきだま ころころ ……………………… 12 ……………………………… The Rolling Snowballs

8　小鳥はどこに ……………………………… 14 ……………………………… Where is My Bird?

9　夕日とブランコ …………………………… 16 ……………………………… Swinging in The Evening Sun

10　小馬と野原を ……………………………… 18 ……………………………… With My Pony in The Field

11　お空をとんだゆめ ………………………… 20 ……………………………… In My Dream, I was Flying in The Sky

12　風とかけっこ ……………………………… 22 ……………………………… Racing with The Wind

13　ささ舟にのって …………………………… 24 ……………………… Sailing in My Leafy Bamboo Boat

14　バレエのおけいこ ………………………… 26 ……………………………… Ballet Lesson

15　花の精のおどり …………………………… 27 ……………………… The Dance of The Fairies Flower

16　鶴のおどり (バレエ "まりも" より) ……… 30 ……………………… The Dance of The Crane Birds
(from Ballet Music "Marimo")

17　エコセーズ—風とポプラのはっぱ— ……… 34 ……………………… Ecossaise —The Wind and Poplar Tree Leaves—

18　メロディ—海辺の子守歌— ……………… 36 ……………………… The Melody —Lullaby of The Seashore—

19　エコセーズ—すずめのおしゃべり— ……… 39 ……………………… Ecossaise —Sparrows' Chatter—

20　ディベルティメント —ペダルをふんで— … 42 ……………………… Divertimento —Go by Bicycle—

21　カプリチョーソ …………………………… 44 ……………………………… Capriccioso

22　即興曲 ……………………………………… 48 ……………………………… Impromptu

練習のてびき ………………………………… 52

54 ……………………… Introduction to the Practice Lessons

表紙装幀／こうのこのみ

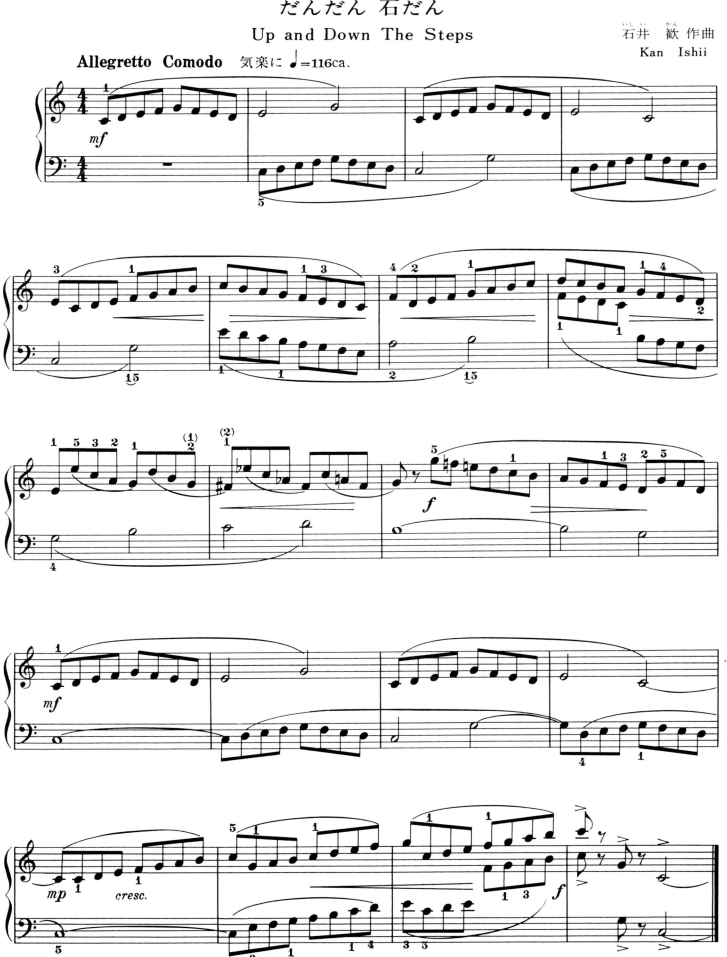

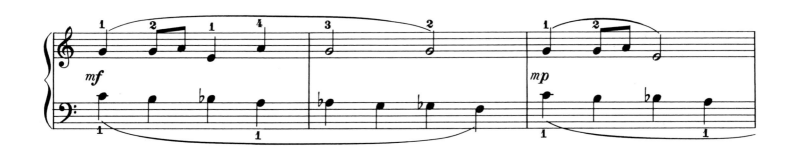

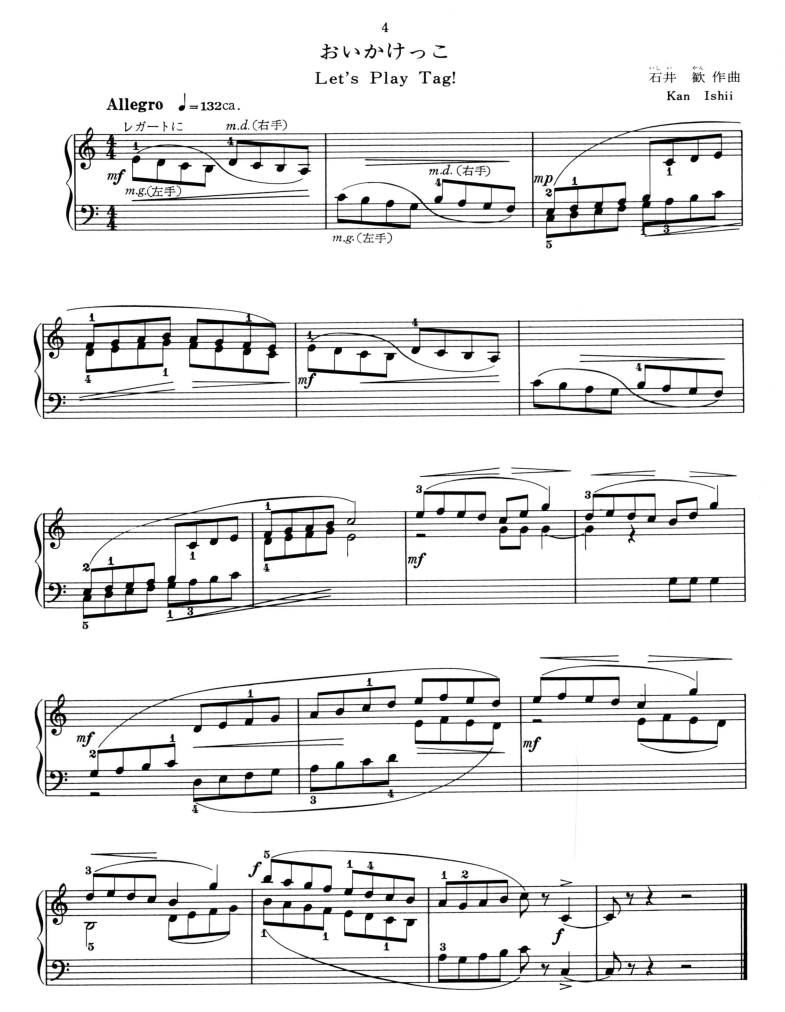

6
小リスのトランポリン
A Baby Squirrel on A Trampolin

石井 歓 作曲
Kan Ishii

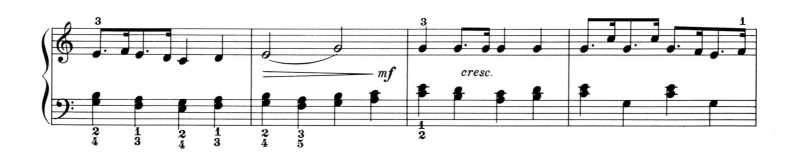

© edition KAWAI

7
ゆきだま ころころ
The Rolling Snowballs

石井 歓 作曲
Kan Ishii

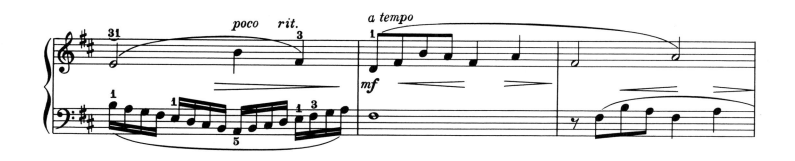

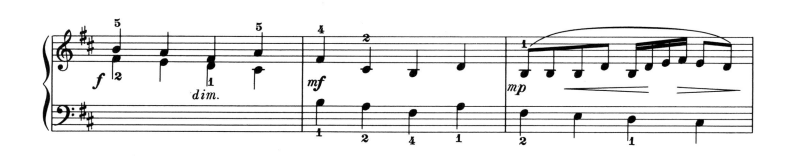

8
小鳥はどこに
Where is My Bird?

石井 歓 作曲
Kan Ishii

Andantino Amabile 愛らしく ♩.=84 ca.

Giocoso たのしげに
a tempo

© edition KAWAI

9

夕日とブランコ

Swinging in The Evening Sun

石井　歡 作曲
Kan　Ishii

Allegretto Cantabile　歌うように　♩=104ca.

11

お空をとんだゆめ

In My Dream, I was Flying in The Sky

石井　歓　作曲
Kan　Ishii

Allegretto Amabile 愛らしく、優美に ♩=108 ca.

© edition KAWAI

バレエのおけいこ
Ballet Lesson

石井 歓 作曲
Kan Ishii

注　※印から4小節間左手は下段を弾いてもよい。

16
鶴のおどり（バレエ"まりも"より）
The Dance of The Crane Birds
(from Ballet Music "Marimo")

石井 歓 作曲
Kan Ishii

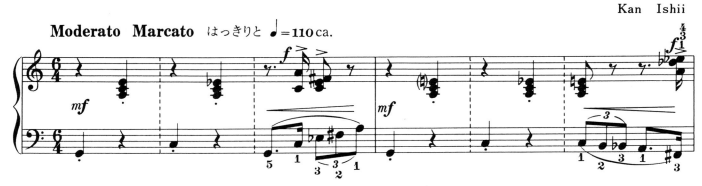

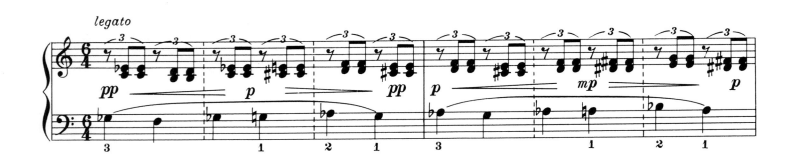
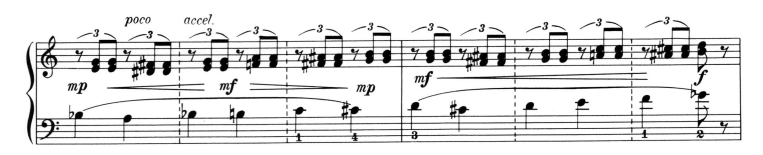

Valse Tempo　Con grazia　優雅に、気品をもって　♩=126ca.

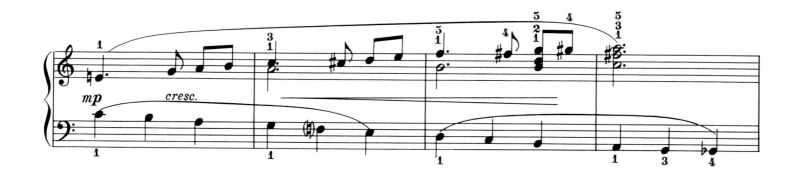

エコセーズ —風とポプラのはっぱ—
Ecossaise —The Wind and Poplar Tree Leaves—

石井 歓 作曲
Kan Ishii

18

メロディ —海辺の子守歌—

The Melody —Lullaby of The Seashore—

石井　歡 作曲
Kan　Ishii

Allegretto Arioso 歌うように ♩=104 ca.

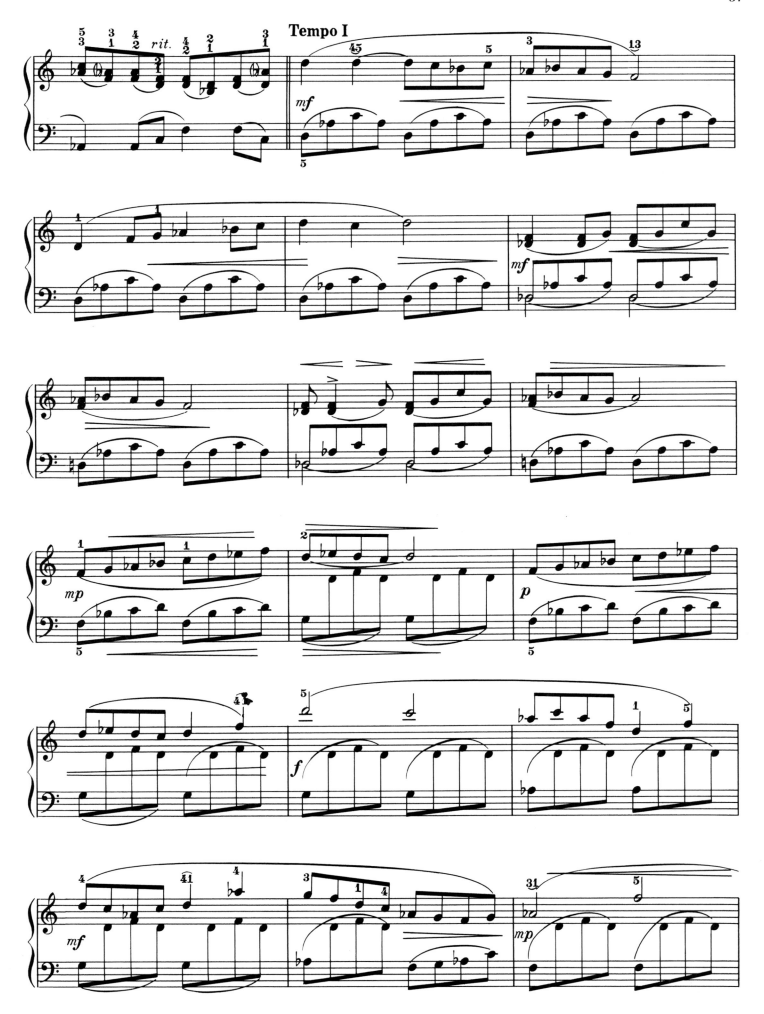

20
ディベルティメント —ペダルをふんで—
Divertimento —Go by Bicycle—

石井 歓 作曲
Kan Ishii

練習のてびき──石井　歓

全曲にわたっての注意

○いつも弾いている音を，自分の耳で確かめながら，美しい音・美しい音楽を創るように心がけてください。

○正しいフレーズ感をはっきりと認識しながら音楽を創ってください。

○その曲の音楽的構成がどのようになっているかを的確に把握するようにしましょう。

○ペダルの多用はつつしむべきですが，和音・メロディの音色を美しく保つように，ペダルの使用法を研究しましょう。

1　小犬とおさんぽ

中庸の速度の2分の2拍子のリズムになれるようにしましょう。

左手の下降するメロディと右手に現れる弱拍から入るメロディとの対比を美しく演奏してください。

2　だんだん 石だん

右手と左手とにカノン風に現れる音型を大切に弾いてください。

13小節目以後に現れるタイの音符に慣れるようにしてください。

3　ゆきみちのおつかい

ひとつひとつの音をていねいに音楽的に美しく弾きましょう。半音階で動く音はレガートで表情豊かに。

4　おいかけっこ

この曲は，右手と左手の受け渡しの練習のためのものです。交互に現れる左手と右手で弾く2小節にわたる下降音階を，よく音を聞きながら一本のメロディになるように，レガートに演奏しましょう。

5　ペンギンちゃんがやってくる

付点をはっきりと軽快に弾き，3連音符と付点音符との違いを明確にすることによって，ペンギンちゃんが歩く様子をかわいらしく表現しましょう。

6　小リスのトランポリン

軽快なリズムを楽しみましょう。

この作品の前半はノンレガート（メゾスタッカート）で後半の同じメロディをレガートで演奏し，その音楽的な相違をはっきりと把握しながら弾きましょう。

右手のメロディの付点を軽くはずむように。

左手の3度の動きは常に音楽的に美しく弾きましょう。

35小節目からは左手のメロディを大切に。

7　ゆきだま ころころ

曲のはじめに現れる右手と，2小節目に現れる左手のメロディの対比を美しく弾いてください。

5小節目3拍目の16分音符は，つぶをそろえて，はしらないで正確に弾きましょう。

14小節目の右手の下降音階と15小節目の左手の下降音階のうけわたしを流れるようになめらかに。

8　小鳥はどこに

この曲でメロディの歌い方を練習してください。

心の中でメロディを歌うように弾いてください。そして左手は重たくなったり強すぎたりしないようにひかえめにメロディを助けましょう。

中間部は明るい気持ちで，クレッシェンド・デクレッシェンドをはっきりつけ，大らかに歌いましょう。

9　夕日とブランコ

メロディをたっぷりと歌って弾きましょう。

曲のはじめの前打音は音楽的に大変重要な音ですからていねいに弾きましょう。2小節目の16分音符の音型は粗雑にならないよう美しく弾くことを心がけましょう。

13小節目からのクレッシェンドを生かして，曲にはっきりとした抑揚をつけて弾いてください。

10　小馬と野原を

軽快な曲ですが，乱暴にならないように。スラーとスタッカートをはっきりと弾きわけることに注意しましょう。

10小節目からは，テンポをやや遅くして，レガートを主体として感じを変えて弾きましょう。

26小節目からの右手の f のテーマは元気よく，しっかりと音楽的に弾いてください。

11　お空をとんだゆめ

左手はレガートに，右手のメロディの邪魔をしないように。

6小節目，10小節目にある装飾音符は弱く美しい音色で弾いてください。

25小節目以後にでてくる16分音符は，テンポ・ルバートで，

やや速めに，レガートにつぶをそろえて弾きましょう。

12 風とかけっこ

この曲は右手と左手との均衡のとれたテクニックを学ぶために作られたものです。

したがって右手と左手とが交替でメロディをうけとる部分が多いのですが，ひとつのメロディに聞こえるように注意して弾いてください。

13 ささ舟にのって

メロディが左手にありますから，右手はごくひかえめに，メロディの抑揚に沿うように弾いてください。

14小節目からは気分をかえてメロディを弾き，左手の拍の頭の音（アクセントの表示のある音）を大切に弾き，表情を豊かにつけましょう。

14 バレエのおけいこ

軽く，あっさりと，バレエの動きを想像しながら弾きましょう。

9小節目からは表情豊かにメロディを弾き，15小節目から小節の頭にあるアクセントの記号に注意してください。

15 花の精のおどり

右手のメロディに対して，左手の動きを表情豊かに弾いてください。

30小節目から4小節間は，上達したら左手の練習のためにも欄外の16分音符の音型を弾いてください。

テンポ・ルバートの部分は，音楽的に許される範囲でやや速めに自由なテンポで。ペダルを有効に用いてください。

16 鶴のおどり（バレエ"まりも"より）

曲のはじめはリズムを正確に，6小節目から強弱をはっきりとレガートで。

ワルツの部分は注意してペダルを用いながらメロディをたっ

ぷりと歌うように。グランディオーソの部分はテンポをやや遅めにして堂々と歌ってください。

17 エコセーズ—風とポプラのはっぱ

音の粒をそろえてリズミカルに，軽く弾いて，強弱をはっきり対比させてください。

中間部・右手の音のきざみは，強さをおさえて，粒をそろえてリズミカルに，左手はメロディを大きく歌ってください。

18 メロディ—海辺の子守歌—

メロディの歌わせ方をおぼえてください。

9小節目からの右手は常にひかえめな強さで，左手のメロディを生かして弾いてください。15小節目から4小節間は，両手共にレガートで弾くように。

19 エコセーズ—すずめのおしゃべり—

軽く，楽しげに正確なテンポで弾いてください。

特に同音の16分音符が不ぞろいにならないように。

13小節目からのテーマは，大きく歌って次第に26小節目のクライマックスを作るように弾いてください。

20 ディベルティメント—ペダルをふんで—

軽いタッチで，リズムを正確に弾いてください。

21 カプリチョーソ

全曲を通じて常にリズムを正確に，生き生きと演奏してください。

中間部は，あまり遅くならないように注意してください。特に，左手の3連音符の頭の音の移動を美しく弾いてください。

22 即興曲

華麗にして大らかな演奏効果を考慮して作曲されたものです。

リズム的な明確さと，後半の大きく華やかに歌う個所との対比を大切にしてブリランテな効果を発揮してください。

なお，再版にあたってcodaの部分をより華麗にするために訂正いたしました。

INTRODUCTION TO THE PRACTICE LESSONS

Kan Ishii

General Information

Firstly, it is important to listen to the tones of your music while you are playing and, at the same time, try to create the sounds with the feeling of beauty.

Play the music with the correct phrasing.

Try to understand the musical formation with each individual piano piece.

Although it is not good to use too much pedalling, learn to use the pedal at the correct intervals to keep beauty of colour tones in harmonies and melodies.

1. Walking with My Puppy

Get used to playing a two-two time rhythm at a medium tempo. There should be a contrast between the left hand melody descendent and the right hand melody which begins with the upbeats beautifully in opposite contrast.

2. Up and Down The Steps

Play carefully the canon form in the right and left hands. Get used to playing the tied notes which appear after the 13th bar.

3. The Snowy Pathway

Try to create musical beauty when you play. Play the chromatic scale movements in legato, expressively.

4. Let's Play Tag!

This is a practice in changing right hand and left hand playing. Play in legato the descendent scales with the right and the left hand for the two bars appearing alternately, and listen to the tones carefully to sound the melody in one.

5. The Penguins are Coming

Imagine the funny way penguins walk. Express its sweetness by giving clear dotted notes in a light manner, and also by giving the contrast between dotted notes and triplets.

6. A Baby Squirrel on A Trampolin

Enjoy playing this light melody. Catch the musical contrast between the melody of the first half which is played in non-legato, "mezzo staccato", and the second half of the melody which is played in legato. The dotted notes in the right hand melody are played lively. The left hand's three degree movements are always played with musical beauty. Play carefully the left hand melody after the 35th bar.

7. The Rolling Snowballs

Create a beautiful contrast between the beginning melody in the right hand and the left hand melody in the second bar. A group of semi-quavers in triple timing at the 5th bar are played with correct time keeping. Play the changes smoothly between the 14th bar descendent scale in the right hand and the 15th bar scale in the left hand.

8. Where is My Bird?

Practise how to play a melody singingly with this piece. While you play this melody, at the same time, try to sing it in your mind. The left hand playing should sound supporting the melody. Try to sound not too heavily nor too loudly. Play singingly the middle part giving "crescendo" and "decrescendo" clearly in a joyful manner.

9. Swinging in The Evening Sun

The melody is played fully and singingly. Play the start carefully, since it is important how the rest of your music will sound. Try to sound the semi-quaver forms in the second bar with beauty and without roughness. This piece is played with distinct intonation using a crescendo effect from the 13th bar.

10. With My Pony in The Field

This is a lively tune, but it should not be played in a coarse manner. Make clear the differences between slurs and staccatos. From the 10th bar, play mainly in legato giving the changed feeling in a slower tempo. From the 26th bar, the f, forte, theme in the right hand is played musically with vigorousness.

11. In My Dream, I was Flying in The Sky

Play the left hand in legato to set off the right hand melody to advantage. The ornaments in the 6th bar and the 10th bar should sound soft and beautiful. The semi-quavers from the 25th bar are played accurately keeping equal timing, in legato and tempo rubato.

12. Racing with The Wind

This piece is to gain a balanced skill in the use of both the right and left hand. Try not to sound the melody brokenly, although the melodies in the right hand and left hand are played in turn.

13. Sailing in My Leafy Bamboo Boat

Since the left hand takes the melody, the right hand playing should be reserved to follow the melody intonation. From the 14th bar, the melody is played with a change of feeling while at the same time being played expressively.

14. Ballet Lesson

Play this piece plainly in a light manner, imagining the movements of classical dance. From the 9th bar, the melody is played expressively. Notice every accent on the first beat in the bars, from the 15th bar.

15. The Dance of The Fairies Flower

Play the left hand impressively in contrast with the right hand melody. When you have mastered the piece, play the semi-quaver form on the bottom lines for four bars from the 30th bar, in order to practise the left hand. The tempo rubato parts are played freely in a faster tempo within moderation. Use the pedal correctly in order to make the music sound effective.

16. The Dance of The Crane Birds (from Ballet Music "Marimo")

Take the rhythm very accurately at the beginning of this tune. From the 6th bar, make the accents clearly in legato. Use the pedal carefully in the waltz and play the melody singingly but with elegance. Play the grandioso parts with a slow dignified tempo and feeling.

17. Ecossaise — The Wind and Poplar Tree Leaves —

Play this piece rhythmically keeping the rhythm in equal timing and contrasting the strong and soft tones clearly in a light manner. At the middle part, the right hand tones are played rhythmically keeping the same timing, however, try to suppress the strength. The left hand melody is played with emotion.

18. The Melody — Lullaby of The Seashore —

Learn how to play the melody with feeling. From the 9th bar, the right hand is played in a softer manner in order to sound the left hand melody effectively. Play for four bars from the 15th bar with both hands in legato.

19. Ecossaise — Sparrows' Chatter —

This piece is played lightly in a joyful manner keeping a steady and even tempo. Especially, the same-tone semi-quavers are played neatly. Play the theme from the 13th bar fully, singingly, and link gradually together with the climax in the 26th bar.

20. Divertimento—Go by Bicycle—

This piece should be played with a light touch and keeping a steady and even tempo.

21. Capriccioso

Always keep a steady and even tempo playing with liveliness. In the middle part, try not to play in a too slower tempo. Play every first triplet in the left hand carefully with the feeling of beauty.

22. Impromptu

This final piece has been composed with much "brillante" effectiveness and with the consideration of its being played at a concert.

	こどものためのピアノ曲集
発行日● 1979 年 7 月 1 日　第 1 刷発行	**音のメルヘン**
2024 年 9 月 1 日　第 24 刷発行	作　曲●石井 歓
	発行所●カワイ出版（株式会社 全音楽譜出版社 カワイ出版部）
	〒161-0034　東京都新宿区上落合 2-13-3
	TEL.03-3227-6286　FAX.03-3227-6296
表紙装幀●こうのこのみ	楽譜浄書●ミタニガクフ
	写　植●創美写植
	印　刷 / 製　本●平河工業社

© 1979 by edition KAWAI. Assigned 2017 to Zen-On Music Co., Ltd.

本書よりの転載はお断りします。
落丁・乱丁本はお取り替え致します。
本書のデザインや仕様は予告なく変更される場合がございます。

ISBN978-4-7609-0506-5